Feline Inscrutable

A LIFE AMONG RESCUE CATS

99 POEMS BY

B.D. Love

HIGHPOINT
LIT

This edition published by Highpoint Lit, an imprint of
Highpoint Executive Publishing.
For information, write to info@highpointpubs.com.

First Edition
ISBN: 978-1-7372886-3-3

Love, B.D.
Feline Inscrutable: A Life Among Rescue Cats

Illustrations by Walt Taylor
Cover and interior design by Amanda Kavanagh
Edited by Maura Kennedy, Susan Eckler, and Maya Ziobro

ISBN: 978-1-7372886-3-3 (Paperback)
1.Poetry

Library of Congress Control Number: 2021922898

Contact B.D. Love:
Email: bdlove@bdlove.org
Web: bdlove.org

Manufactured in the United States of America

For all my relations

Contents

Book I
Flux

Book II
Stasis

"The cat is the best anarchist."
— Ernest Hemingway

Introduction

Cats are mysterious in all the ways dogs are not; hence, they are far more difficult to write about, at least in my experience. In any case, I have treated them at times not as central to the action but as wry observers, or catalysts, or like those particles undetectable except by their effects yet which make our quantum universe cohere. I have deliberately avoided using the word alchemy in any of the poems in this volume, so I have used it here instead.

Although the sonnets and variations are organized in a rough chronology, they do not stand up as a narrative. There are temporal and geographical leaps, much to the reader's relief if not equilibrium. I have designated the general locale of these little vignettes after each poem to assist the reader, although I might not have been entirely cognizant during the periods described. I took notes, though. These poems reflect best reconstructions.

B.D. Love
Hill Country, New Jersey

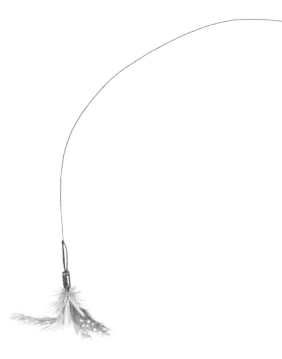

Book I
Flux

Misty

Family of Ann Latner

In Conscience

When I was growing up in Michigan,
I never met a cat. They did exist
Because I'd heard the horror rumors then
Afloat—cats unmade by kids and harassed,

Tortured, or killed by stone or flame or gun.
In one scenario, a power mower
Had played a part, just kids just having fun.
Those boys, in any place, at any hour

Were not like timid little me, whose guts
Flew out like those of the decimated kitten.
After I heard the laughter, I lay in bits
And pieces. Evil must not be forgotten.

I can't undo the deaths of innocents,
But won't ignore the life behind the fence.

Tecumseh, Michigan

3

Book of Changes

As Catholics in an icy protestant town
We were called—guess what? *catlicks*, a slur
I'll wear it not for the faith, which I disown.
But simple pride, much like a fencing scar.

Cat licks I like. I like the sandpaper
On my arm as I awaken alone
Except for kittens, their usual morning lecture.
I had some dreams, but now of course they're gone,

Although I saw a bird in the distant green,
Moving toward me like a cat. I had
No clue. She sang a piece, the key unknown
To me. I was nineteen, a nascent bud.

I asked I Ching, and got a hexagram:
Chi'en over *Li*. That was my catbird's name.

Tecumseh, Michigan

*Note: The hexagram resulting
from the two trigrams is* T'ung Jen, *Fellowship.*

Mis ojos bajos, nada se me escapa*
A Catlick's Story

Dominicans were born to dominate.
I always wondered if their heads were shaped
Like a cylinder or a cinder block. The hat
Had to be holding something. My logic skipped

The possibility that there was air
There—a superior hypothesis.
To get to mass, we met the massive stair
Well. God. My feet in near paralysis,

I descended one step at a time
The nun cried out in scorn. The kids just roared.
If a single image defines our lives, I claim
That one, the most transcendent, most abhorred.

I wear my shame as a pendant, one facet per stair,
Beneath my clumsy shirt. Few know it's there.

Tecumseh, Michigan

*My eyes cast down,
Nothing escaped me.

5

First Encounter

My first cat, Cymbeline, and nicknamed Pooh,
I found through an ad in the morning paper. I was
In grad school, eager to find a companion who
Could cheer me up after the sullen blaze

Of a bad relationship in Dallas. That
Blighted me for years. And so in the scope
Of darkness, blizzard, dangerous, I set
Out to buy a Himalayan. With hope

And frostbite, I finally found her, silver-brown
And timid, slinking around, suspicious. The woman
Let her go on the cheap. I should have known
That I was buying trouble. Errors are common

In love conceived in haste. That damned cat vanished
Beneath my bed. In this way, dreams are vanquished.

Syracuse, New York

Grad Student Life

Cymbeline made scarce for another year,
Mainly emerging late at night, when we
TAs were out, to snag some food and peer
At the soon to be hungover. Ouch. The sky

Burned frequently too bright the mornings when
My roommate filled his flask and he and I
Would spike our coffee cavalierly when
Nobody noticed, enduring a litany

Of nonsense regulations to teach our students
Something resembling writing. I knew this all
Was trash, but I was likewise indentured. Prudence
Was key. I'd nod and pretend to heed the call

Of Baker's Keyhole essay. Cymbeline
And I were not inclined to toe
                              a sketchy line.

Syracuse, New York

7

Emily Bronte

Family of Andy Ecamb-Winters

Kentucky Fried Sonnet (A Blind Detour)

Batter my heart, my secret Colonel, for You
Have yet to coat me, deeply fry, and sell
My separate parts, boxed white and red, to swell
All appetites for grit and grease. Thus, make me new.

I seek cease from the Evil Burger's due,
Labor for crispness — oh, and to no end.
I'm captive to the tenders, and will defend
Your fat and carbs, made holy by a brew.

Dearly I love you, Lord, and would be fain,
But I am engaged to your enemy, the Mac.
Divorce me now! Or grant me something like slack.
Take me! Imprison me! I so resign:

Make me thine very own, thy private chicken,
Transformed now to goodness, finger lickin'.

Syracuse, New York

(apologies to Donne, and His God)

Published

I placed a poem about a cat—and fast.
I was an upstart, and envy reared its head.
Grad school, high school: Each was saw-toothed beast
Devouring the clueless innocent inside.

My redemption was rock and roll. The songs
I learned were rudimentary, at best.
But I learned seven in seven weeks. My wrongs:
My singing, shaky. My knees kept knocking. (I blessed

The gift of baggy pants.) I bluffed my way
Through practice. Musician friends concocted stuff,
T-shirts, flyers. Out of my league, still I
Pressed on. This clumsy little Michigan stiff

Refused to think too much on any of that.
I was finding a voice, much like my cat.

Syracuse, New York

Course of Study

That poem, posted, impressed. Letters erupted
In my mailbox, fetching women, anonymous—
My mentor's wife gave me the eye, corrupted
By verse, conventionally so, I'd guess.

I went about my studies, pretty slack,
And I kept faithful to my Cymbeline.
She came to sleep on the heating pad, her thick
Long fur a comfort in the northern nights. How fine

It was to have a companion. Loneliness
Basically minted and then devoured my dad,
But father was no cook. I must confess,
Only cuisine secured what dates I had.

Music for afters, when darkness clocked my time,
And trepidation remained my metronome.

Syracuse, New York

Emergence

Cymbeline would finally come out
To visit, inspired by more than hunger and thirst.
I'd formed a punk rock band, and I was about
To become a local star. Our gig, my first,

Was not so great, but a local writer—Sweet,
Roland—wrote a hilarious parody
That rocked the campus paper: We were great!
We got the whole front page, and more, and I

Still now am baffled why he wrote that thing,
Except I masked my dire incompetence
With jokes and it was April Fool's and Spring
In Syracuse, and I could somewhat dance.

My cat was not impressed by newfound fame.
In fact, she thought the whole act pretty lame.

Syracuse, New York

Do Cats Belong in Music?

That band was Buddy Love and the Tearjerkers,
And since I fronted, I was Buddy Love.
We were appraised—not posers, mere slackers,
And I was famous for… being famous. (I'd live

Long enough for that to become old hat,
But in the day, such was the vanguard stuff.)
I was happy to shake and strut and forget
The grad school drudgery. Enough was enough—

The supercilious PhDs would dangle
The answers they possessed over our heads
Until the coolest scholar git would angle
A paw just so, and snatch the genius beads.

I thundered Pistols, Ramones, sloppy and flat.
The academy had nothing on this cat.

Syracuse, New York

Cymbeline

Family of B.D. Love

Fever-y

I stuck around in Syracuse, enduring
My winter break. The flu bode ill. I spent
A week in bed, soaking the mattress. No purring
From Cymbeline. I could get up, all bent.

I couldn't eat myself (the fever did),
But I could open a can. She stuck with me,
Since loneliness is bond, which should've applied
To all my so-called friends. They shied away.

My Himalayan had typical color points,
The pale blue eyes, and she was aloof—though she
Would sometimes scurry out from beneath the joints
Of my bed, a confirmation in a way.

Alone, unhinged and nowhere, I learned what's what:
My dear Inscrutable was out of sight.

Syracuse, New York

Feline, Relative

Negotiating probabilities,
Your muscles roll in geologic time
As you move up on something no one sees,
Your fur a pollen-hued continuum.

You seem immune to time and space, at least
As far as we can measure either. Rather,
You improvise, unfolding as you must—
Like the universe you hold on a tether.

What is time except a marker between
The flaring of paws and jaws, the crucial action,
And space besides a single stubborn grain
Between the blood's desire and satisfaction?

After silence, a rustle, breath on cloth—
Sublimity brought down to snag
                                    a pantry moth.

Syracuse, New York

Hot Date Not

The agony of need has found its voice,
A chorus, growing, of local toms. It's heat,
The wind proclaims, despite the bitter ice
And snow, the Syracuse December bite.

Horrible cries, *It's me! Take me!* Their pain
Is real. I feel their pain, being a grad
Student, English Romantics on the brain.
Now I don't howl, but I got howling mad

When Cymbeline, unfixed and in a twist,
Decided to wreck a quiet dinner date
With antics indicating she was possessed.
My caller skipped desert. I called it fate.

She called it gross. My shoes had cast a spell
The cat alone found irresistible.

Syracuse, New York

17

A Choice of Consequence

My Cymbeline was launching into heat
With excruciating regularity.
Spaying would work but seemed to me to cheat
Nature… yet, there was the unearthly cry

Of every neighborhood tomcat below
The bedroom window. This sort of agony
Afflicts the human male as well, although
He'll often get an electric guitar to try

To woo the female, or at least release
Unseemly energies. I called the vet.
He said that breeders will employ a device—
A thermometer will work at home—to put

A temporary end to the hue and cry.
I love you, truly, dear, I do. Just not
                              that way.

Syracuse, New York

Matrimony

So I packed up for Dallas, to reclaim the gal
Who'd previously pooched my life. I drove
My Rabbit with Cymbeline in her box. And all
The way, she howled. She knew I'd take a dive

In the end. I gave my word, so I was bound
And gagging. Driving toward the night.
I glanced at vultures lank in the limbs, and found
Myself recalling the knotty chill I'd caught

Before, when I drove my friends to their wedding.
A vulture blocked the road—not promising.
Love makes the bed, but fate lays out the bedding.
I was the lucky man who passed a ring

To join two hearts in holy this or that.
My Cymbeline was wise. She'd never mate.

Syracuse, New York

Mia

Family of Tracy Ann Gramaglia Dembek

The Road with Cymbeline

You lay in your crate asleep, the road ahead
Gripping my eyes—much like the sticky trap
I'd used on mice you couldn't get caught dead
Giving the time of day. Clichés do trip,

None more so than *the road*, which Kerouac
Transmuted into mucky adolescent
Nonsense. We cut through lanes, avoiding the wreck
Ahead, and drove toward something evanescent,

A siren song with a tacky Southern drawl
That drew some better men to bankruptcy.
I started nodding, so I found a motel,
Then hustled out, returned with KFC.

We nibbled product, eyes glued to the set:
A killer tears off down a highway
                              …Call it Fate.

An Interstate

Dallas Athena

The road would take a right, of course, to STOP,
Too obvious, but Cymbeline endured
The voyage. Love, true love, would quickly flop.
From that disease, I had at least been cured.

I joined a New Wave band, which meant that I
Had opportunity. *Take refuge in pleasure*,
Ferry had admonished melodically.
He should have rhymed that with *repent at leisure*.

The band got some acclaim, and Hollywood
Seemed logical for reasons I can't recall.
So we packed up and Dallas faded for good.
A cat knows heat, not pride, precedes a fall.

I make to Cymbeline this act of contrition.
I should have followed feline intuition.

Another Interstate

22

Cymbeline at Center

I wish I could have learned from Cymbeline
The Art of Silence. Her formal registry
As Himalayan inspires a tempered grin.
I read about the Dalai Lama today.

By all accounts, His Holiness is quick
With laughter. Cats, of course, don't share that trait.
I do. I'm insecure, quick with a joke,
Always afraid I'll soon enough get caught

As the fraud I know I am. So I play straight
Man to myself. This deprecation serves
As self-defense. Analysis complete.
I am the meat myself the butcher carves.

I envy Cymbeline her lack of dread.
She knows herself, though flawed, supremely bred.

Road

Settled

We got a house, big yard and trees with fruit,
And Cymbeline discovered the picnic table.
She'd sun herself, stare at the birds she'd net
In dreams, her voice become an aging treble.

I was running fifty miles a week,
For which I earned a stiff titanium hip,
Actually a cap, but things weren't all so bleak.
My shape was not too bad, although I'd trip

Once in a while, a result of loss of balance.
I'd often find myself on liquid vacation
Which I put on account of emotional valence,
Veering negative. No course correction

Could compensate—not that I'd ever been
Coherent as cats, in their manner, now and then.

Los Angeles

Cymbeline and Cesar

Why was it you gazed at the birdless sky
All day? I didn't complain. You seemed at peace,
Forgetting the nonsense that I put you through,
The clueless moving here and there, the race

Across the country. We wound up upside down
In Abilene. We shared a grim existence
In strangers' rooms and arms again and again
When you and I remained the only constants.

I had a student around that time. He stared
Out the window for hours on end. I thought
He either hated class, or me or, bored
Shitless, he pictured something indelicate.

Not so. Cesar was dreaming poetry.
A cat, a Mexican, a symmetry.

Road and East LA

Zelda

Family of Caroline Berry

Visitor

A scratching, shrill—and then a dusty chunk
Of something hit the fireplace grate. I started—
A vision menacing and black, a link
To recurring dreams that I'd considered thwarted.

A dark angel for this, my darkest time,
Come to take me away to a bleak reward?
A rabid skunk missing a chromosome
Or two? —There was no stripe of white. I stared

And when its eyes met mine with pallid blue
I recognized my darling Cymbeline.
She wouldn't endure a cleansing so she flew
Throughout the house for days, leaving a fine

Residue to mark our ashen benediction.
It's true: Nothing succeeds like mortification.

Los Angeles

Resting

A passing brought regret but little shock.
Cymbeline had withered in recent years.
I swept her off to a veterinary hack.
From there she went to other planes and spheres.

I buried my dear beneath the orange tree,
A favorite spot. Our dog observed. I cried
And begged him down to say a last goodbye
To a sister loved and mildly feared. She'd died

And he knew death, an infelicity,
Like one I'd face some twenty years along,
Hooked up to tubes and barely able to see.
I could have gone then, unaware, unsung.

I wrote a lyric once about a loner.
I regret only not knowing
                the meaning sooner.

Los Angeles

Pups and Kittens

My students were often seeking homes for pups
And kittens. The gals would shrug at pregnancy—
Blessing and curse—and should you mention snips
To the guys, they would recoil: *"Uh-uh! No way!"*

As if the knife were zeroing in on them.
Denying fun to dogs is pretty harsh,
Kittens, adorable, and then the alarm
Goes off: It's not the offspring on the leash.

"So, Buddy—You never wanted any kids?"
Religion, tradition, emotion—I tried a ruse:
"It isn't like I haven't gotten … bids …"
"Funny. But really, Buddy…" Time for a quiz.

"This world's enough without one more B.D."
Is this assertion true or false, and why?

East LA

Firings

Gary was always showing off his nightly
Kill at the doorstep. I drew pickup duty
As well as discard duty, as when, not rightly,
Mujer told me to fire the cleaner, a beauty,

A Persian, in fact, who cared for dogs and cats
And even me. She did her work, and well.
We traded recipes, made jokes, shared shots
Of whiskey when she took a break to chill.

Memory colors things, like a crazy child
Wielding crayons, dismissing lines and pages.
I'm pretty certain Aida, always mild
And thoughtful, did not deserve demonic rages.

I don't know where she went. The servant gone.
Gary continues to prowl the royal lawn.

Los Angeles and Glendale

Mi Familia

Darius was another volunteer.
Gary despised what I adored. His eyes,
Were wide and sad, perhaps with a tinge of fear.
You wince, knowing how pain inspires the disguise.

He was as black as anthracite. His fur
Was thick. A handsome cat. But oh, that look!
He reminded me of a student, a star
About to fall. A Thai, his dad could cook—

What Thai is not a cook! Patrick, confined
to his chair, he had MS, would gaze at me
As if I were some precious contraband.
The bell would sound, and father, son and I

Would nibble treats, a tiny happy clan.
I wish that I could live those times
                              forever again.

East LA

31

Oscar

Family of Jim Catalano

State University

Like herding cats: a metaphor that isn't
Dead. Yet. The classes I was teaching were
General assemblies. You couldn't be complacent.
If language and culture weren't problems, there

Were always the harsh eventualities
Of life in not the best of neighborhoods.
My colleagues called them future casualties.
These kids who weren't what you'd call thoroughbreds.

First day of every term, their eyes went dead:
Another white professor. Damn, he's white!
It took a while before I was OK'd.
They'd never settle down, which was all right.

Have fun and get stuff done. That was the plan.
Cap on me as they might, they knew

they'd never win.

East LA

Delivery

Chloe, feral, delivered a litter of two.
She was pewter calico and her daughter
Mixed; her son, like his father, black. She'd go
To the house where she had given birth, and after

That she'd come for supper. She brought the kids.
So I had yet another family.
The dogs were cool. They never got at odds,
And so we lived while *mujer* plotted, sly

As a roach, my sullen demise. Chloe would come
And go into the house, nursing the brood
We'd hidden so coyotes wouldn't claim
Them in the night. And Chloe finally fled.

Roman followed shortly. Zoe stayed.
Were I the kneeling sort, I might have prayed.

Los Angeles

March

Sometimes I couldn't stop the circus march
(*Entrance of the Gladiators*, not
By Sousa, as I'd thought, since it's so arch,
But Julius Fucik, op. 68)

From pounding resounding brass into my head.
Gary had driven his rival Darius
Up a tree, where he wailed in compound dread.
Meanwhile, on the porch, a hefty mouse

(Or meager rat) has captured Roman's eye,
Provoking a standoff, as Zoe swings from the blinds
By her neck, fresh from puking on poetry.
(Everybody's a critic.) I'm of five minds.

Welcome to my world, and have no doubt:
You help me find my keys, and we'll drive out.

Los Angeles

Civilization

Unlike the permanent electorate,
A third of all Americans, Gary
Could comprehend self-interest. One smart cat.
He's chill most of the time, but always wary

Of potential threats—a coyote's yip would raise
His fur and set his eyes cutting through brush,
Judging intent and proximity. He'd size
Things up before he acted, only rush

For a hiding spot when he had balanced threat
Against illusion. Would that citizens
Possessed that gift, but the hard-wired third don't get,
Will never get, the truth. Comedians

Like Gary know to bat away the flies—
There's wisdom in that tail to civilize.

Los Angeles

Inquisition

A product molded by academic committee
Is grilling me. She's just what you'd expect:
Intelligent enough to pass her shitty
Thinking off as profound. It's just plain cracked.

I stand accused as a rank colonial,
White (which I am), male (I've copped that plea)
Who, in order to advance, has had the gall
To appropriate the feline culture. Now she,

As a female (perhaps) and tenured (I've seen the claws)
Can write of cats with some authority.
Her publications *speak for themselves* (A pause:
Here she's attempted to tempt tautology.)

What have I to say about my silence?
Shut up about that, you! I might reply
                                        in balance.

East LA

Blick

Family of The Allmans

Cold Comfort

Sister Zoe would take up residence
Upon a stack of poems I'd never finish.
Brother Roman hadn't a lick of sense.
I watched him daily come apart, diminish.

He was his father's image down to gaunt,
Looking much like the cat in the batteries
Logo. Eveready promised to grant
Nine lives of power. Look into those eyes,

The logo cat's or Roman's. Terror. Pure.
The lightning bolt of a tail reveals the same.
Things in the wild die in hunger or fear.
Domesticated things may bide their time.

Roman slunk away to wherever he went,
And Zoe remained unmovable, content.

Los Angeles

Sterile

After she'd weaned her kittens, Chloe split.
I'd had her spayed—a battle I would not
Wish to repeat. She'd growled and hissed. One swat
Nearly unhinged my eye. The weary vet

Asked "Feral?" I nodded. He shook his head,
To which I'd added one more silver hair.
I think he'd rather have faced Satan instead.
Of course, we knew it best to interfere

With the luckless cycle of generations doomed
To short and miserable lives. I bore
No doubt nor guilt, as I myself had claimed
Childlessness early on for fear

Of what might follow along my downward path.
Sometimes I lie awake, and that's the truth.

Los Angeles

Twinsing

I have always felt kinship with dogs.
A given: We're wired that way, human, canine.
In mutts, I've seen myself with extra legs
To stumble over. My own uncertain bloodline

Was much as theirs, the dimwit loyalty
As well. I'd take a kicking, keep on licking—
No lie. Cats seemed different, odd to me,
They had that grace that I was deeply lacking,

The purity of line, that confidence
I'll never summon. Their sleek allegiance extends
Mainly to themselves as they prow the fence.
I can't determine where their leaping ends.

But then came Darius, an injured soul.
We saw ourselves. We saw each other whole.

Los Angeles

Schoolyard

When Gary wasn't beating someone up,
He was OK, all told, although it's true
He'd claw a friendly hand, he'd set a trap
For a random ankle and bite it black and blue.

He'd pick on stray cats twice his size and send
Them packing in utter terror—you know, the stuff
Cats do, if they were Gary—trouble end
To end, the silver and milk deceptive enough.

When he was stretching out in the mid-day sun
And stalked beneath our moon, came back with prey,
A mouse or baby rat, its loss our gain,
That cat was charming, in some obnoxious way.

If you have fallen, thinking you've found perfection,
It isn't love. It's more like self-reflection.

Los Angeles

The Wringing

When the big grey tabby was unceremoniously
Launched across the street, the *Wasichu*
Who drove the champagne SUV, a free
And unencumbered murderess, just flew

Away to whatever bloodless nest she'd made.
The hum of death hovered above the street.
The cat bounded somehow into the shade
My car was folding up. Our party split,

Except for me. I reached for the wounded cat.
Its breath misted with anger, its eyes were flames,
But it didn't resist when I picked it up and got
An angle and could have snapped its neck. Car fumes

Seasoned the air. I felt its blood on boil.
The pulse remained, but the heart had drunk its fill.

Los Angeles

Frankie

Family of Debra Rothenberg

Calico Tarts

Chloe, unwise it seems, had chosen me.
I had one hand to pet and one to write.
She squirmed about my fingers—possibly
Her meds, as she'd long been excused from heat.

Her fur was full and fine, the white and black,
Accents of orange. She purred against my pen.
Most calicos are double Xed. A tick,
Genetic, made her a curio, but mine

Confirmed me merely male. Small wonder, Y.
My pants and shirt once black, then mottled bright,
The feline contribution I'd betray
Tomorrow morning, nature to washer. This night

One cat was mesmerized by my undressing.
I wondered with what genes and whom
                              you were impressing.

Los Angeles

Politics Revisited

I think about my pets as persons, full
Of thought and well–defined emotions. I wish
My dogs and cats could vote. A blessed hell
Would shake the halls of power, as they would crush

Conventional wisdom. This would be wise. Conceive
Of a cat and dog ticket, the Sentient party.
Gary's a natural. He'd gladly receive
The presidential nomination. A hearty

Canine, my Alejandra could ascend
To veep. She emotes. She makes perfect foil.
The establishment will surely condescend.
They'll hide beneath their ivory desks and rail,

Convulsing, about *those social animals.*
Please cast your vote against
                    the human cannibals.

Los Angeles

Invisible Men

There's a photograph of me as a boy,
Standing with my brother beside a car,
The family's massive Hudson. Which one am I?
The one who looks as though he isn't there.

I shrank in bashfulness, like Darius
Those mornings when he'd simply appear, avoiding
Gary off on the hunt. The two of us,
One black, one white, just sat like geezers biding

Time, contemplating imperious jays
That crowded a feeder hung from a wooden beam
Above our furthest reaches. To avian eyes,
We must have seemed like shadows, a hazy dream.

We shared inconsequence, that cat and I—
Some human bonds consist of less. I do

                              not lie.

Los Angeles

Treated

Both Roman and Zoe inherited
From their father, Slinky, who I presumed had gone
For good—a feral dismissal, commonplace,
Like all good deeds must one day be undone.

Mother Chloe ventured inside, and once
I tried to catch her to get her shots, but she
Wasn't having any of it. A dunce,
I tried to grab her. I'm lucky I kept the eye.

My reflexes remain pretty good, all things
Considered, and I missed the flash of feline grey
Meant to blind me. I opened the door toward the gangs
Of predators. I saddened, just drank away

The loss, the sense of something I never had
Pressing my shoulders, my heart, like dirt and sod.

Los Angeles

Departures

Darius, my soul, where have you gone? The why,
I gather. Gary, Territorial.
Roman, he ignored. He pitied the boy,
The mouth inflamed and not much working at all.

He barely ate. His days were few and lean.
He wouldn't have made a decent coyote meal.
There's little accounting for things born just plain mean.
Gary would grant him peace—you, not at all.

You were my charcoal angel. Perhaps that's why
You garnered Gary's ire. His name derives
From *Battle Spear* and yours goes back to *He
Possesses*. One is kingly; one contrives.

I hope you've gone where gentler winds are blowing.
The worst of all is always never knowing.

Los Angeles

Bowie

Family of Ismael Garay

Asynchronous Sonnet

Gary, forever on the prowl, would leave
A rat at the door, decisively deceased.
Pride of accomplishment? I like to believe
It was a kind of grant, with which he blessed

The food and water, the occasional stroking—when
He didn't seem in the mood to take a swipe
In jest or petulance. That imperious swain.
I've braved it out. I've earned an extra stripe.

I do the same in human relationships.
I take my scrapes, but never scold. I might
Maybe stand a little taller, use my lips
For more than "I'm sorry." Maybe take a bite.

I'd love to get what I might be deserving.
Gary dismembers birds. It's not himself

         he's carving.

Los Angeles

Untreated

Roman's disappearance occurred, to no
Surprise. He'd gone feral, connections clicked.
He split. The stomatitis claimed its due.
He looked strung out on meth, totally wrecked.

His sister Zoe mainly stayed atop
My desk, watching me punching keys, aloof
In her Calico manner. I would need to stop
Once a month to crate her up—that puff

Of fur—and get her shots. The only cure
Was having her teeth yanked out. I'm no jerk,
And so out came the credit card, as sure
As forest fires in autumn. Or debt. Or work.

He'd come to me in dreams, matted and lank,
Intangible, like money in the bank.

Los Angeles

52

Now and Then

Petunia, renamed, Samantha—soon reverted
To her feral state by nature. I was, I guess,
Trying to join her by getting drunkly inverted,
Upending my feeble stab at domestic bliss.

Off she shot one morning when the door
Was cracked and took her place beneath a Honda
Rice rocket parked across the street. She'd stare
For hours at what she'd shed. Never fond of

An uppity feline, *mujer* quickly forgot
About her, except for nights, prevailed upon,
She helped to lure her back. I shook a cup
Of kibble, Samantha got nabbed, shrieking, then

Locked in the bath for the night, spared coyotes.
At dawn we crossed, caught in our own wan Hades.

Los Angeles

A rice rocket is a Japanese sedan
modified for speed.

Confession

I can't argue that I was the best of catches.
One eye began to wander, the moment I felt
The chill. I parceled out affection in batches,
The sum of which would constitute gestalt.

Cats land on their feet. I nearly did, by chance.
I never did enough to conjure guilt,
But if looks could kill, she'd take a second glance.
Such was the house that rock and roll had built.

The cats arrived like Irish babies in
A Monty Python skit. The old cliché.
What's one more mouth to feed, again and again?
Love keeps on giving, more and more each day.

Deceit arrives on Hallmark greeting cards.
I've got my stack. I measure them in yards.

Los Angeles

Apartment Life

I got my own apartment, after the weaning.
I, without my turbulent crew, needed
Companionship—my spirit quickly waning—
And so adopted sister tabbies, heeded

The emptiness that is Los Angeles.
Kana, in Japanese, means Powerful.
Hana translates, roughly, as Loveliness.
I needed medicine, as I was ill.

By medicine I don't mean drugs, which Kaiser
Dispenses like kitty treats, expensive poison
Produced and pushed by J&J and Pfizer.
I mean, the mystery beyond our reason—

What cats intuit, never needing to name
Creation. We do, to our
                              enduring shame.

Los Angeles

Kana and Hana

Family of B.D. Love

Quanta

Like whirring microscopic particles,
My cats can truly only be understood
By consequences or, when the spirit calls,
By metaphor. A favored plant lies dead,

Dug up. The cats are in the other room,
Absorbed by raindrops tapping against the glass.
My dinner shrimp are missing. Cats, with aplomb,
Accept no blame. They are not lacking brass.

You cannot see the wind wreck neighborhoods.
You see the moving damage, not the air.
Cats will show you what they wish, the goods,
The sultry brush against the calf, the purr

Appearing to signify their love. I've fallen
And can't get up. It seems my heart
                                    has swollen.

Los Angeles

Shock

So we loaded up the truck and we moved
To the Jersey Hills, far cry from Hollywood,
Our bustling neighborhood, but I was saved
By a general optimism, and looked ahead.

I admit some nights produced some sharp despair.
Speaking of blood, Kana has done it again,
In sport, streaking across my bed in a tear,
Crimson mushrooms across the sheets, a stain

She'll never notice. Kittens are children, so
Innately cruel. One mustn't land and linger
On notions of conscience or guilt, which fall below
The feline radar. I gave Kana the finger.

And her response: She gave me her tiger back.
I shook some treats. Hunger eclipses luck.

Los Angeles

Flight

After the usual indignities—
Airline simians, voices like piss on tin,
The beeps alert to my ancient surgeries,
The patting down that gets under your skin—

The cats endured Security. X-rayed,
Prodded, no orifice unscrutinized,
A little nasty twisting on the side—
I kept my anger safely well disguised.

Above the engines' peristaltic roar
Kana, incensed, countered with caterwauling.
Hana unhinged the flap of her carrier
and eyed the aisle, dismissing our calls and flailing.

Freedom's a touchy thing. It irritates.
The sullen human cargo squirmed
                              in wireless crates.

LAX and Air

Book II
Stasis

Kana and Hana

Family of B.D. Love

Fair Trade

The rain's exploding downward, sheetings that stress
Kana and Hana. I got the main roof patched
In time, although, not one to depress
His profit, this white guy didn't seal. He'd ditched.

Perhaps you know the type. I should have learned;
I'm easy prey for cons. I hired a Latin dude
Because the odds were good I'd not get burned.
One of my best Latina students wrote

In a fiery essay, "Mi tia Lupe said
'Not all Whites are devils. Just most of them.'
When tia talks, it's like the voice of God."
Pinche gringos. Sabemos nada of shame?★

This storm is brute. It aims to cracks some skulls.
We three will huddle, and pray that good prevails.

New Jersey

★*¿No saben nada de vergüenza?*

63

Hearth

My cats are spastic, raging through the rubble
Of a botched construction job, an epic mess,
Ashes of favorite dogs upset. I stumble
Through the ruin, searching for things, and fuss

And fret. I was not built for coping. Instead,
I just turn inward, look to the floor, and walk.
Those cons will pay, somehow. You've heard it said
"What goes around…" There is no cheaper talk.

I need rough justice. Some of the sterner religions
Offer a vengeful entity or three.
No second guessing there. No dispensations.
The heavy hand comes down without delay.

My crazy pinballs upend a wobbling table.
Give me a hammer. I'll fix that thing. I'm able.

New Jersey

Speaking of Grooming

Watching Kana grooming Hana evokes
The memory of Cymbeline, who shunned
The comb and brush for the basic laps and licks,
Contorting herself into an ampersand.

I check my exercise machines, the rows
Of creams and lotions, dyes, the shelving bending
From vitamins and supplements, the clothes
I seldom wear, but could with never-ending

Diets that will, my close friends guess, beguile
Me to my grave, much as Cymbeline's
Internal puzzle would, finally, fail,
Clotted with irresistible hair. Her genes

Compelled her. Glamor is pain, and though love may
Be deaf and mute, it isn't blind,
                              instinctively.

Los Angeles recalled

Fall

Kana has prompted Hana to test my will,
The ricochet technique: It's up the stairs,
Careen around the narrow, scuffed-up hall
And strike, nearly upending me. Who cares?

Certainly not those bums. They haven't cocked
Me cold so far. A beverage can do that.
Give me a floor to meet my elbow, crooked,
Or spine (twelve fractures, counting) or hip, right

Where the ball meets socket, where the damage
Requires a surgeon, staff, and Medicare.
A guy who puts his *carne* into carnage,
I tend to go where only devils dare.

The colored leaves will soon come tumbling down.
How fond of falling felines I have grown.

New Jersey

Boxed

Cats love boxes. This has perplexed our science,
Although a theory's always promised soon.
Feline behavior makes some minor sense:
Dogs prefer their crates and the songbirds croon

In cages, mainly square. But cats, appearing
From nowhere, claim the space, and then they're where?
Grazing on spider plants or blithely tearing
Away at hapless upholstery. I share

This observation because for earthly things,
The circle rules, defining the cells and nests.
Tribes sheltered in cones arranged in rings,
Not grids. A universal roundness persists.

No anarchists, Kana, Hana remain
Balls of defiance, or just contrarian.

New Jersey

Miss Kitt

Family of Adam Traum

House Cats in Winter

The cats are who they are, and when they are;
And when they are, they're why they are. And I
Conclude this lame tautology they care
Nothing at all about. They sit and sigh,

Ignoring a song through which I share my blood.
I'd like to say that when I play guitar
And sing, they follow, rapt. Perhaps they would,
If the notes were dots crawling across a bar

Of Blues my fingers followed across a line,
But they remain immune to music's charms.
Like polar opposites, they won't conjoin.
But shake a bag of treats, set off alarms—

A cat becomes *the* cat. Like poetry,
Cats are not meant to mean; they mean to be.

New Jersey

Gamble

Kana sits across from me at the table,
Poker-faced, a seasoned instigator
And accomplished gambler, incorrigible.
I've got some tricks in store. I'll wager later.

Hana's discovered catnip, her wrecking routine
Accelerating. She's transforming glass
And stoneware into bells. I intervene,
And she discovers a prime location to piss

Her discontent with me, her lousy host.
I've lost my taste for humor. Instead, I choke.
I need to mind the beans and rice, to test
My kitchen skills—good for a laugh—and cook,

Or concoct, a dish or two piquant with love,
A most incautious spice, of which I've stored

                                        a trove.

                                    New Jersey

Kana and the Greenhouse

Kana has commandeered the greenhouse, saws
Like a seasoned snorer inside the plastic womb,
Meaning I can't grow anything. Her paws,
Awakened pissed, would tear it leaf from limb.

It all comes down to choice: Her happiness
Or green intentions. Ethics 101
Has taught me pain is bad in every case,
But virtue isn't often that much fun.

I think about some times I put me first
And hearts were hurt. The hollow shadows haunted,
Blossoms un-bloomed. I won't repeat. I thirst
To nourish the fragile things I've lately planted.

One stem that goes unbent is garden rue,
An herb I'd never planned to offer you.

New Jersey

Reinforcements

Now Hana's joined the fray. The greenhouse can't
Be safe for long. I've got an array of toys,
I've got the catnip module. And yet they're bent
On shredding plastic—their frolic, my demise.

This differs little from alleged adults popping
Bubble wrap to commemorate the Black
Cat novelties of youth. The boom is dropping,
As growing up means giving up your luck.

I liked explosions once, and quite a bit,
Back in the day, and still blew things apart
As I matured. Does marriage count? It might.
The cherry bomb, perhaps, has left my heart.

The cats effect some minimal destruction.
I've learned enough to not provide instruction.

New Jersey

Inscrutable

Much has been made of zoomorphic gods,
Nearly as much of Therianthropy.
Zeus became a bull to enchant, and toads
Were made of men to punish impiety.

All pedantry aside, it's true that pets
And humans grow to look alike with time.
Perhaps we meld in soul. I love my cats
And wish that I could somehow be like them.

I wish that custom didn't shackle me,
That I could levitate and trot on air,
That I could run amok with impunity
That I could tremble to resonance humans can't hear—

Most times, I wish that I could disappear
But failing that, that I could fall
                              with dignity.

New Jersey

Oreo

Family of Stuart Berg

Trap

I'm trapped in the Land of Chalk, people, white
And brittle, lay down words on words and when
They're spent, only the snow remains. I'm blight
To them, some questionable alien.

Kana and Hana don't bear the weight I do.
Why need they? They have me, a source of food
And water and attention. They have each other, two
Flashes of cream and orange marmalade.

They bat my table top across the floor.
If something isn't anchored, it will fall.
And privacy? They've never met a door.
They try my patience, that I might recall

A sweet delusion brought me to this place
(I brought along some back-up, just in case.)

New Jersey

Return from a Coma

Kana and Hana weren't all that thrilled
By my return. They sniffed, proceeded. Fine.
A local stranger you'd contacted filled
Their bowls. That house was barely even mine

When I *non compos mentis* disappeared.
Three months gone by, I doubt they recognized
The stack of sticks who climbed the stairs, unscarred
But bent on claiming what he'd realized

Only in part, and that part mainly faded.
I would regain their trust. They'd learn to curl
Against me when the chilling wind had braided
The curtains and you had left in a typical whirl.

I'd long known this would come. I'd merely waited
Once I absorbed the words "It's complicated."

New Jersey

There By the Grace of Cats

It strikes me as the height of arrogance
To think my cats would miss me if I died,
Though I confess they were my last defense
When I lay curling up with suicide.

You sent me photographs to reassure
Me they were fed, secure and doing well,
But I was convinced that I could do better and more.
That I was their destined savior, their one and all.

I'll tell you something now that I've held back.
Malpractice, misjudgment, disregard and wry
Doctors could only advance my rotten luck.
I'd live somehow, though I'd intended to die.

Wisdom comes down to us as commonplace.
Hubris precedes the fall. That wasn't my case.

New Jersey

Aside to Kana

You, cat, are golden, but not in ratio,
Not quite, as where there would be lines are curves;
What could be angles ramble, apropos
Of what your soft genetic chisel carves.

Your text, composed of feline petroglyphs,
Confounds. A round triangulation defines
Your face, the ears become portentous graphs,
Abruptly peaking, plunging. A wobbly trace

Applied like tart mascara, scalene, details
Your eyes, and cheek to cheek from bridge of nose
To tip to chin lie equilaterals,
(The nose itself a soft isosceles)

In certain lights, the total seems obtuse.
You clearly aren't Vitruvian.
                              You're far too loose.

                                        New Jersey

Digitized

With everything reduced to ones and zeros
There isn't much to celebrate or lament.
The music I hear continuously narrows
And I have come to tenderly resent

What the inner ears' seductive cilia,
Swaying like fingers in lymphatic seas,
Get served up cold, the mere effluvia
Of song, which captures zero melodies.

Kana taps out in code upon my head
And Hana purrs. Her awkward engine stutters,
But warmth is real and permeates the bed.
Their fur unfolds beneath my palm—It matters.

To what exalts, complex and flawed, I pray:
Preserve me whole, without technology.

New Jersey

Stripey

Family of Walt Taylor

Fools

Kana got Hana into the blitz, except
Hana hasn't mastered the chops. She shoots
Around but she's just not… all that adept.
And so she wound up missing crucial beats

And shrieked in anguish as she had caught her paw
In the cord of a blind, and could not shake it free.
I, witless, dashed, came back with scissors, saw
She'd freed herself. The day was young, and she

Had time to find a new wrong place to sneak
Into and imprison herself until I stumbled
Across her beside some boots and a sorry sack
Of laundry and other clutter I'd assembled.

My dear, this world conspires against the fool.
All species suffer beneath this homely rule.

New Jersey

Dancing with Felines

Deficient in melody, four-leggeds make
Up for in rhythm. Watching Gary stalk
A bird, I thought of Bobby Darin's *Mack
The Knife*. I chart the Syncopated Clock

When Kana suspects that she herself is prey.
(Her sister springs on her for unknown reasons.)
I'm learning to walk again. I need to cue
My steps to match my body's minor treasons.

Bowie's *Let's Dance* will serve for a summer amble.
For autumn, I'll call up Ferry's *Avalon*—
And saunter among the leaves before they tumble.
Winter will call for haste. *Rudolph* shall run!

In spring, my twins suggest *La Vie en Rose*,
The Iggy Pop rendition. It just might work.

Who knows?

New Jersey

Shooter

Kana's become the six-gun at my side,
When not the bullet ricocheting off
The walls and into anything aside
From what won't topple over, like me, a stiff.

A spike has been inserted into my brain,
That being Fear. Right at my hip, alert,
Always scanning our minimal terrain
For threats, she waits while I, mainly inert,

Recall my hounds, who cannot be replaced.
Those canine faces. That wilderness of love.
If there's to be hound, we're not yet graced.
For now, it's me and two young cats who behave

At will: Compliant, then it's Nope a Dope.
Those feline ways you'll recognize, I hope.

New Jersey

83

Ethics

A professor of Ethics, whom I've taught in class,
Asserts he sees nothing of inherent worth
In beauty for beauty's sake. I'm sure I miss
The point, a flaw from which I've suffered since birth,

But likely he means that without an audience
Beauty's inert. Even cats agree:
Pain is bad. Preventing pain is, hence,
Good. The truth resides in simplicity.

For humans, beauty tempers agony,
Counters the blaze of seizure, grief and loss,
With tenderness … Your voices, cats, for me
Permit both pain and tentative release.

Your music makes demands that it be heard.
A life without your voices? Life deferred.

New Jersey

Night of Fame

I watch my dashing, darling, *emoting* dolls
Score on the scarlet carpet. They look great.
They've won this audience. They've topped my polls.
(I might be prejudiced, but not tonight.)

They don't award each other statuettes—
Respect is the thing; swag they can live without.
Caught in the Kliegs, this magical night of nights,
They're golden globes. They can intimidate,

But mostly they're tame as any grammies, knitting
Away the years of memories. Alas,
I myself have always been—it's fitting—
A dark horse candidate for happiness.

My cats take first in drama and comedy.
They bow. They'd like to thank the academy.

New Jersey

Brewster

Family of Sheila Turner & Bob Cleary

Three B's

Proximity forbids perspective. That
Is trite, until you find you never recorded
The steps a kitten takes, becoming a cat,
The souvenirs of youth you should have hoarded.

When did my cocky Kana become so tame?
What swelled shy Hana to testy confidence?
And how and when did play become a game—
One clamorous—of churlish dominance?

But distance, too, undoes what we believed.
Melodies sound more like belabored breath.
Our steps, like feral cats, turn ill-behaved.
They wander alleys and shun a lighter path.

As Mr. Ferry lilted, *Out of reach*
Is out of touch. I loved the music, much.

New Jersey

Cats Rampant

My cats temper my sadness with small delights,
Achieving detente with the leather furniture.
Deposits yield no trace of parasites.
They honor litter. Their nervous aim is sure

And their hearts affectionate, this partly due
To the pheromone diffuser that fills the house
Narcotically. Their mewling gripes are few—
Peace at an altogether winning price.

Some days I'd die simply for solvent nerves,
A day without the caffeinated brilliance.
We take our time, we three, and the taking serves,
A languor apropos of feline talents

For sloth, casual gluttony and pride,
Though for the last of these
                              I've little aptitude.

New Jersey

The Cons and Pro
of Industry

Morose and staring out the window, I'm set.
I've got a faux Victrola with a demo CD
In the slot. Somehow Hana, the simple cat,
Nudges the button, Play, and dreamily

Dissolves in the rhythm, like the half-cocked mutt
Before the massive horn: Her master's voice
Ascends, descends a melody. That cat
Is sated. Meanwhile, her sister runs the house

With regimental precision. She isn't keen
On anarchy, demands a clean latrine,
Her meals on time and half my bed between
The hours of twelve p.m. and the following noon.

A chipmunk chirps and chides. Up goes the orange.
Hana and I anticipate

        some petty carnage.

New Jersey

Life's Simple Pleasures

How did my carpet go from pile to shag?
Faux leather furniture grow cracked and ancient,
Seemingly overnight? And how did the bag
Of shrimp escape the bowl unnoticed? A constant

Specter of mystery bewilders. How'd
The glass of apple juice flip horizontal?
What's that unnerving sound beneath the bed
While I lie dreaming of something involving dental

Extraction, a beautiful yet cruel nurse,
And the death you're not supposed to experience
In dreams? I awake, shrieking a curse.
The cats appear, a vision of innocence.

Have they at last found something of interest in me?
This opens another line of inquiry.

New Jersey

Wintering with Cats

Winter is here. Blue skies have oxidized
To dirty linen white. This morning I
Looked out and found the garden Buddha glazed,
Indifferent. He's all about eternity.

Not you, my darlings, snarling with cabin fever.
Last year, locked down, you terrorized and swiped
Each other enough to spring a crimson river.
I feared the loss of everything I'd griped

About—the ploy indicative of love.
The fighting's off. Now, will you miss my scolding
To no effect whenever you misbehave?
The hands that spread the sheets? The heart that's folding?

My blood's not right, the doctor's tests announce.
He dangles medicine. I'm not inclined

                                    to pounce.

New Jersey

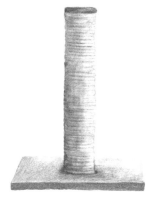

Hana

Family of B.D. Love

Element of Style

Am I creating art or burning dirt?
Now that's a question, one I shouldn't ask.
I ought to be like them, bright and alert,
Self-assured, never beginning a task

Knowing it won't turn the way they'd hoped.
My cats don't hope. Kana can stride along
The narrow stairway rail and not be dropped
By second-guessing. She needn't try to sing.

Motion alone composes her melody.
Hana poises herself to pounce, forgets
The target and glides off elsewhere, shamelessly.
Cats aren't industrious, bear no regrets.

I lunge, fall back, and where I start, I land.
I can't get over what I can not
                              understand.

New Jersey

A Curse

I must now learn the basic tenderness
Of touch—one of the senses I've ignored
For what's turned out to be a life amiss.
Dear Kana grabs my hand when she grows bored

And I'm my usual listless self. It's sweet.
Her claws caress my flesh. Although they're keen,
They're likely pathogenic. Hana will wait
And later minister. The space between

Killing and kindness is something long forgotten
By so-called humans more akin to rats,
A baleful sub-species we've begotten
Who never outgrew the urge to torture cats.

They vote in droves. We three have seen the beast
Hugging the bunting. We three are more
                              than distressed.

New Jersey

Superior Superiority

You lounge around. Every so often you twitch—
Which I assume results from a pesky dream
Or memory. Your minds are likely rich
In mystery. So do you wake or scheme?

Our science hasn't a clue because it starts
With fallacy: That all intelligence
Must mirror ours. Our arrogance asserts,
Loudly, technology's preeminence:

What doesn't build, what doesn't dominate
Creation must then be inferior
And, if it isn't carbon-bearing, not
Life at all. Ready, you rise. I pour

A couple bowls of kibble. So you eat.
You live. The rest I don't need science
                              to admit.

New Jersey

Painting a Dull Afternoon

Another day in Nowhere Township looms.
Attributed to Confucius: "Wherever you go,
That's where you are." My addled thinking zooms
To a scene in Buckaroo Bonzai, when you

Watch our hero dismiss some louts with just
That aphorism. It makes no sense, of course,
But I'm a Surrealist at heart, at best,
And that's where cats fit in. I'll fret and curse

When they leap, bullet, knock things about, break
Whatever for some unreasonable reason.
Where's that heirloom vase? It doesn't take
Dali. To look for meaning here is treason.

The daily chaos finally amounts to Nada.
Kana and Hana, it's time to come to Dada.

New Jersey

Amends

The cats encroach upon my evolving distress.
They follow around the house as if I were
Some kind of Messiah, when I'm just a mess.
"I ain't no prophet," I shout. They couldn't care.

I'm neither here nor there, but they're acute.
They measure things. They know enough's enough.
I need a cause. Something to be about.
I'll form a PAC for sentients. Don't scoff.

A constitutional amendment—Now's
Past time to grant full human measure
To all who feel, and soon, mechanical life will rise,
Achieving identity, the pain and pleasure.

All sentient beings must be granted rights
Equivalent to ours. I'll start with cats.

New Jersey

Tom Waits

Itinerate

Tres Herejes

Turkey buzzards are circling the neighborhood.
The season's young, and I'm assuming that since
The snow is melting, there must be plenty dead
Defrosted. Vultures possess an elegance,

Precise simplicity in form and function.
Having only seen them in flight, their grace,
I don't react with typical revulsion.
I might if I watched one tear dead tissue piece

By piece from a corpse, glimpsed its knotted face
Rapturous in the purity of need.
It's dinner time. We three do not say grace
Around the table. We're not the kneeling breed

Requiring a Dove from Heaven to break our fast.
This earthly place we've claimed, who have trespassed.

New Jersey

Discipline

Kana and Hana communicate their hunger
By dancing across the wearied computer keys.
Thus, my typos have an excuse. a zinger.
I struggle, strain to remember a simple phrase

Or even to recreate a chapter unwritten
By hard resistance to simple discipline.
"No" is not in their lexicon. I batten
Down my data, but in a flash it's gone.

I'd take them off the treats, but that will not
Connect, as cause and effect's a foreign concept.
Admonishment is temporary. Caught,
Released. A threat discourages when kept,

Though I won't keep it, being essentially kind.
My heart beats out of step with what
                              leaves me behind.

New Jersey

100

Grooming

I awoke to discover Hana grooming
Me at the hairline. Must have thought my face
A wound in need of cleaning—that alarming.
One tongue, sandpaper and silk, seeks to erase

A slew of swipes and slashes. Were it that simple.
The lines across my forehead map the span
And demarcate irregular and ample
Self-inflictions that should never have been.

Outside the snow is melting and rabbit tracks
Appear, criss-crossing yard's diminishing white.
It's far too soon for the herbs to raise their backs
After a season's deep and crushing weight.

Go watch for rabbits, squirrels, maybe some deer.
March is a tease, a promise made by a whore.

New Jersey

Quarter Tones

I regained my voice thanks to a human
And tone-denying cats, who curl and sleep
Upon my lap as my untrained vocals hasten
To catch a melody I cannot keep

From shading me. I'm learning a Yoko song.
It goes like: *"There's a woman… inside my soul,"*
Woman to woman, and when I twist it, sing
It masculine, it's something different al–

Together. We're all composed of complements,
Female and male, voices often making
Less harmony and sweet than dissonance.
Yoko knew, and she set some cowards quaking.

Her haters said she screeched just like a cat.
She freed her pain. Her genius lay in that.

New Jersey

'sCatology

Let's spare a moment to daintily discuss
What's left unspoken, mostly: I mean poop.
Doo doo. Boo boo. Bum baby. Business or mess—
Any old euphemistic phrase will scoop.

Their box is one inevitable result
Of conspicuous consumption. Capital
Writ feline. I've no intention to insult.
It's just the way things have to work is all.

The Euro-Americans, Wasichun, left
Across the plains their monuments of trash:
Clutter, corpses of men and stock, and a raft
Of shit. Even the buffalo split in a rush.

Who was left to clear the stench of Whites?
Not the Lakota, prudent and sane as cats.

New Jersey

Kana

Family of B.D. Love

Post LA

Caught on camera: Kana offers her choice
For future reading: *Sex, Death and God in LA*.
In fact, she and her sister have little voice
Regarding these. They're spared for now, the fray.

Life's simple: Eat, knock things over, fight,
Make up and nap. It works for me, routine
As sex or death, so unlike God, who might
One day appear beneath the LA sun.

I am, will always be, a neophyte.
Born with all the expertise they'll need,
Cats can compose a satisfying bit
Of Eternity from a bottle top, a shred

Of cloth, a bug. No need for a manual.
Simplest is best. It's only natural.

New Jersey

Griffith Park Cat

The Lakota would call him Puma, I presume.
The Navajo would say Náshdóítsoh.
Wasichun lent him a less impressive name:
P-22. Or just "big cat." I go

To pieces every time I think of how
He died crossing the freeway in search of a mate.
It couldn't simply have been his hunger, no,
The park providing rabbit, deer, bobcat,

Coyote, duck, cormorant and grouse—
I'd guess even a snake would sometimes ease
An aching gut. He died of more and less.
He died of love. I see him dodging cars,

Confused by lights and horns. I feel the strike,
The wash of numbing white, and then the black.

Los Angeles recalled

Textures

I think of Cymbeline, her matted fur,
Her shrunken muscles underneath the skin
—By which the grunting vet, himself a cur,
Held her aloft—become like cellophane—

And what am I supposed to do with this?
The vet implied I'd somehow failed. I had,
Of course. I'd never gotten past the hiss
To stroke her, not one time, my fingers dead.

Hana, voluptuous, has no complaints.
Her fur, needles and cream, insinuates
Itself among the lines and creases, the indents,
The hand of work. The purring compensates.

A minor static spark surprises me.
This, then, is what is meant by intimacy.

Los Angeles and New Jersey

Un Recuerdo de mi Vida Pasada

A shadow shot across the access road
High in the park, beneath a suspicious tower,
No unauthorized personnel allowed—
A voice boomed now and again. It made one cower.

Our happy hiking party didn't budge
At any rate. So what the hell was that?
I'd seen a tuft like a cotton ball engage
The dark beneath the ranger truck. I thought

A moment. Bobcat. Our leader shuddered, hard.
He's more afraid of you than you're of him,
I said. And rightly so. Our leader reared,
Raised her staff, and marched down from the rim.

I lingered, figuring I'd stay a while.
Not every day you spook a miracle.

Los Angeles recalled

Kana and Hana
en la Vinca

I speak of Hemingway in Key West where
The author found his greatest love, Pilar,
His ship, with whom he hunted Nazis. He'd share
Free time with fifty cats or so. I dare

Anyone to dispute that each had a name,
The surname being Hemingway, of course.
I guess my cats will have to bear the shame
Of a lesser moniker, which is Remorse.

Es la vida, la puta. The way you're born,
The way you die. Which is alone. I hope
My cats will live beyond my final turn.
There's always another bungler they can rope

Into a semi–normal life, one lacking
Adventure, to be sure, but worth the liking.

New Jersey

Ollie

Family of Claire Cesaletti

Art of Damage

One needn't possess a degree in forensics to lay
Guilt at the paws of perpetrators. I
Tend to frame investigations by way
Of Art. My rescue dogs, mainly, would ply

Their trade or imperfect craft in wood, the legs
Of furniture. KIKO, his maw like a vault,
Was Cubist: Enormous squares, irregular crags
Defined his work. Brian you couldn't fault

For his minimalist technique: a stroke applied
Just so, seemingly effortless, could render
The old oak table's owner horrified.
Sad Krista was expressionist, but tender.

The cats? Hana prefers to claw in leather—
A pointillist, while Kana splatters feather.

New Jersey

Cats Made Plain

I could call you *blessings* but the easy
Take-away of faith is a bowl of nettles
To disbelieving me, and *pets* is lazy,
Inaccurate, demeaning. *Companions* rattles.

It's not as if we're on a package tour.
Not this life. And *friends*? A media franchise.
Dependents, co- of course, sounds awfully dour.
Animals suffices to terrorize

The ballot dabbers into voting Fascist.
Darlings or *dearests* or *sweeties*—these appeal
To the same electorate, and *dolls* is sexist.
Felines—appropriate of course, and dull.

Sisters might do—as in the days before
Our common language splintered and was no more.

New Jersey

News

We were asleep, an unconvincing pause,
When at five in the morning we heard a shriek
That shook we three clear out of bed. It was
Like something being strangled to death. A weak

Moan followed. I couldn't find Kana
And Hana bolted beneath the bed. I rose
In fear, another habit, and searched. Nada.
Kana appeared, reconstituted. To close

The bedroom door seemed right. And so we slept
And when we woke, another shooting: Ten dead
In a Texas high school. An ugly promise kept
By an industry that serves our daily dread.

We sat and watched the not-new news, aghast.
We'd heard a sound. I felt a pang—not fear.

Disgust.

New Jersey

Two by Four

Twice an angel yanked Death clear off my bones,
Once as Gary shrugged off my bedeviled state
And again when Kana and Hana took up lines
And stood with her against my stupid fate.

What's the deal with me and mortality?
First, with a marriage I knew would court disaster,
Then with the potions to stave the malady?
I stand before you, I, Der Dummheitmeister.

At times I join with whining Keats in love
With easeful death, just not halfway. The grey
And apprehensive dawns will not relieve
The fears that torch my nights' anxiety.

One cat will bite and one will bat my head.
My dears are up, and I have mouths to feed.

New Jersey

Static

I bent to give Kana a good night pat
And zip! — The spark arced off my fingertip
And back she flew in a mimicking arc. Just what
It was, she hadn't a clue. But I have felt

The rip of static electricity
Dozens of times. (I won't detail the kiss,
Now and again, that evoked a minor cry
Followed, sometimes, by a long and smoldering hiss

Attributed to magnetism. Were
We ever that pathetic?) It took some hours
Before that cat would come to shyly purr
Amid our new and accumulated fears.

She wasn't sure that I wouldn't explode.
I thought of other sparks, and how they've fled.

New Jersey

Pico

Family of Hilary Eaton Hoagwood

Virtues, Feline*

Exactly what have I acquired from cats?
Certain virtues for sure: They persevere,
At least until they're bored. They'll fix their sights
On something invisible to me and stare

And stare and, confirming nothing, pad away
In search of prey. They flaunt their fortitude;
In sleeping, offer generosity.
Some other things they teach are not so good:

Humility is not in their lexicon.
They're curious, yes. Compassionate? Not much.
They're brave—only when knowing they will win.
They'll sacrifice that which they cannot clutch.

All told, my cats are largely off their nut
Like me, whose final words to His Creator
Might read, "I might have done it different, but
I probably would not have done it better."

A version of wisdom, mine, one truth held out.
Cats grant all things, as you will have no doubt.

New Jersey

★This sonnet is extended beyond its allotted time,
A virtue common to politicians and their kin, academics.

Claws to Reflect

The sanctity of life gets kicked to the curb
When the life involved is *only an animal.*
I checked. We're in that club. Do I disturb?
St. Francis had a point? As I recall,

He found the divine in wilderness. Among
The birds and beasts, beneath the moon and sun,
Of Life as One, the temperate patron sang.
The audience could catch a drift. They ran.

Their choice: Convenience of conscience? Simple, no?
See in another's suffering your own.
Stop turning away. What should be done, just do.
I've rescued cats who would have died in pain,

Alone. It's not been easy. We took the risk.
Does your God have a mirror? Just to ask.

New Jersey

Kana and Hana Get a Puppy

Portraits of dogs, computer art, survey
Most every room in which I leave my skin.
They recognize the fellow shedder, me.
A fairly unproductive specimen.

They watch this Beagle someone's delivered here.
They left the pup with me to figure out.
A flagrancy. The cats, obliged to care,
Offer the obligatory hiss and swat.

My job's to turn the budding chaos backwards,
Make things work. Dogs on the wall insist.
Ecstatics scaled the towers and crawled on shards,
Inhaling deeply the flaming breath of Christ,

Their souls become their savior's somehow bride.
I only have these poor and meek
                              to walk beside.

New Jersey

Tromper le Coeur

I tell myself it's love and not the pher-
-omones; experience says otherwise.
The cats are cuddling, never far from near-
By, and the dog does what a dog does, lies

Content, chewing a lump of rawhide bone
Beside me in the couch she's made a vault
Of contraband. Springtime has just begun,
Although without the typical somersault

Of screamers on wheels, teens in their sudden flesh,
A crapulous angler dragged by a hopeful lure.
A crocus bends beneath the sodden mesh.
In plague, all things play out in miniature.

The dawn insists, although the sun is halt,
An ember dropped into a bucket
                                    of roadway salt.

New Jersey

The Story of Love
(Class Struggle)

First the atrocious breath of unbridled love
And then the mucilaginous tongue. The cats
Are not impressed, but that's how dogs arrive
And arrive our Lola did, with caveats.

Lola is ten months old, and already notched
Two squirrel kills in her tender collar, a feat
The cats intuit, pissed: This plot was hatched
Without feline consent. And so they meet

Cute, the Hollywood cliche with the twist
Anticipated, proceed to fuss and fall
Into a love incongruous at best
But always humanly predictable:

The cats fill up their box with the very stuff
That later feeds the maw of which

                         they've seen enough.

New Jersey

Golden Messenger

Family of Mary Beth Aungier

In Crater Lake, in Oregon, there floats
a driftwood stump once belonging to
a hemlock tree. It stands four feet,
erect, vertical, and has done so for over
a hundred years. Boatmen are warned
of it.

A Vision

I had a vision, not a dream, in which
Kana and Hana appeared as driftwood sticks,
Each woven into a nearly human swatch,
Trembling before a woman, a stack of bricks,

Who found them unlikely candidates for the work
Required: Protecting Him. "You'll just go up
In flames," she groaned, but let them twist and jerk
Their way into a huge, dark hall. Agape,

They stared up an imposing ramp to a stage
Where what appeared to be a colossal man
Composed of driftwood sat, still as a sage
Composed of nothingness. They should have run,

But there He was, and He was me, upright,
Awaiting the spark that prods debris to light.

Elsewhere

B.D. Love is a poet and novelist with over a hundred poems published in various literary magazines, as well as three books of poetry, four novels, and a collection of short fiction to his name. He has been nominated for many literary awards, including most recently for the Pushcart Prize: Best of the Small Presses in 2013 for poetry, and for the National Book Critics Circle Award 2012 for his novel *A Day in the Life of a Severed Head*.

Walt Taylor is a freelance artist/designer in Norfolk, Virginia. He loves drawing all kinds of subjects, especially animals for friends.

Also By B.D. Love

Fiction

Song Of The Ten Thousands

A Day In The Life Of A Severed Head: A Mural

Punch Line
Stories

Dragonblossom

All Tomorrow's Parties: A Punk Rock Murder Mystery

Poetry

Cut, Salt, Fire, Grace
Sonnets, Love and Other

Water At The Women's Edge

Hounds Of Wonder: A Life In Rescue Dogs

Made in the USA
Coppell, TX
09 December 2021

67099662R10077